THE STORY OF ROY CAMPANELLA
Campy

by DAVID A. ADLER

illustrated by GORDON C. JAMES

Viking

VIKING
Published by Penguin Group
Penguin Young Readers Group, 345 Hudson Street, New York, New York 10014, U.S.A.
Penguin Group (Canada), 90 Eglinton Avenue East, Suite 700, Toronto, Ontario, Canada M4P 2Y3
(a division of Pearson Penguin Canada Inc.)
Penguin Books Ltd, 80 Strand, London WC2R 0RL, England
Penguin Ireland, 25 St Stephen's Green, Dublin 2, Ireland (a division of Penguin Books Ltd)
Penguin Group (Australia), 250 Camberwell Road, Camberwell, Victoria 3124, Australia
(a division of Pearson Australia Group Pty Ltd)
Penguin Books India Pvt Ltd, 11 Community Centre,
Panchsheel Park, New Delhi – 110 017, India
Penguin Group (NZ), Cnr Airborne and Rosedale Roads, Albany, Auckland 1310,
New Zealand (a division of Pearson New Zealand Ltd)
Penguin Books (South Africa) (Pty) Ltd, 24 Sturdee Avenue, Rosebank,
Johannesburg 2196, South Africa

Penguin Books Ltd, Registered Offices: 80 Strand, London WC2R 0RL, England

First published in 2007 by Viking, a division of Penguin Young Readers Group

10   9   8   7   6   5   4   3   2   1

Text copyright © David A. Adler, 2007
Illustrations copyright © Gordon C. James, 2007

LIBRARY OF CONGRESS CATALOGING-IN-PUBLICATION DATA IS AVAILABLE
ISBN: 978-0-670-06041-2

Set in Berkeley
Book design by Jim Hoover
Manufactured in China

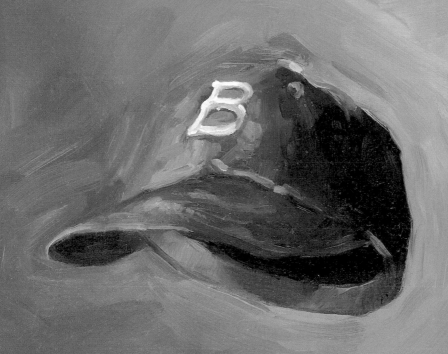

For my grandson Jacob —D.A.A.

To my wife Ingrid for all her love
and support during this project. —G.C.J.

The Los Angeles Coliseum was dark. More than ninety thousand fans had come to see a baseball game on the night of May 7, 1959, and about halfway through the game, the lights had been turned off. In the darkness, the fans stood and lit matches, a silent tribute to Roy Campanella.

"The sight was electrifying," Campanella later remembered. "The Coliseum suddenly burst into a mass of blinking stars. . . . I've never seen anything like it."

The crowd that night was one of the largest ever to see a baseball game, and on each admission ticket was printed, "I was there the night they honored Campy."

For Roy Campanella, their beloved "Campy," it was a long journey to that night of tribute.

Roy Campanella was born in Homestead, Pennsylvania, on November 19, 1921, the youngest of John and Ida Campanella's four children. His father was an Italian American. His mother was an African American. When Roy was seven, his family moved to Nicetown, a section of Philadelphia.

Segregation was widespread in the 1920s. There were many stores, theaters, parks, restaurants, and neighborhoods closed to African Americans, but Nicetown was a mixed community, a comfortable place for the Campanellas.

Roy Campanella's father sold fruits and vegetables and awoke at five each morning to load his truck. Roy got up, too, and helped. When he was twelve, Roy took a job delivering milk, and had to get up even earlier, at two in the morning. Still, he came home in time to help his dad.

After school, when the weather was good, Roy and his friends were outside. Mostly, Roy liked to play stickball, a form of baseball played with a sawed-off broomstick and a small rubber ball.

Some afternoons he sat on the roof of a house just outside Shibe Park, the home field of the Philadelphia Athletics, and watched Major League Baseball games. He loved the sport and decorated his room with pictures of his favorite players, Babe Ruth, Lou Gehrig, Satchel Paige, and the great catchers, Mickey Cochrane, Bill Dickey, and his hero Josh Gibson—"the black Babe Ruth."

Roy was big for his age and a good athlete. He played baseball at school. He also played for a team of boys sponsored by a Philadelphia newspaper, and soon on men's teams. He was a catcher like Josh Gibson.

As catcher, Roy crouched behind home plate with the whole game in front of him. He studied the other team's batters and then signaled to the pitcher what sort of pitch to throw. He was good at calling pitches, and a powerful batter, too. Soon he was known as one of the best young athletes in Philadelphia.

In the 1930s, baseball was a segregated sport. African Americans were kept out of the Major Leagues. They played instead on teams in the Negro Leagues. One of the best was the Baltimore Elite Giants. In 1937, at the age of fifteen, Campanella joined the Giants.

He spent just about the entire summer of 1937 either on a baseball field or on the Elite Giants' bus. He played as many as four games a day and traveled at night from one city to the next. He ate, dressed, and slept on the bus.

Later that year, on November 20, 1937, the day after his sixteenth birthday, he quit school. "To do that," he later wrote, he knew he "should at least be grown-up enough to go into the world and earn his way." Campanella felt he could do this, as a full-time professional baseball player.

He played over the next several years on the Elite Giants, and on teams in Puerto Rico, Mexico, and Cuba.

After the 1945 season, Roy Campanella met with Branch Rickey, president of the all-white Brooklyn Dodgers system. "Your record is good . . . a hard worker who loves baseball, a man who gets along well with people," he told Campanella. "Play for me."

Campanella thought he was talking about creating a new Dodgers team in the Negro Leagues, but he wasn't. He meant one of the many white Dodgers teams in the Minor Leagues, maybe even its top team, the Major League Brooklyn Dodgers.

One week earlier Branch Rickey had signed another African American, Jackie Robinson. Rickey wanted to get the best players he could for the Dodgers, no matter what their race. And he wanted to end the segregation of baseball.

In March 1946, Campanella signed with the Dodgers.

That spring, one middle-level Minor League Dodgers team refused to take Campanella, because he was black. But the one in Nashua, New Hampshire, was glad to have him.

Roy Campanella loved baseball. He didn't pay attention to the ugly racial shouts from players on other teams or from people in the stands. Words didn't upset him. He just enjoyed the game. But physical attacks did bother him. When one player threw dirt in his face, Campy warned him to stop or "I'll beat you to a pulp."

That year Campanella was the leading catcher in his league in throwing out opposing runners. He was one of the top batters, too. His team won the league championship and Campy was voted the league's Most Valuable Player.

In 1946, Jackie Robinson played for one of the Dodgers' top Minor League teams, the one in Montreal, Canada. In 1947, Robinson moved up to the Brooklyn Dodgers, the first black player in the Major Leagues, and Campanella moved up to the Montreal team.

In Montreal, Campanella excelled. He was again voted the league's Most Valuable Player. Campy joined the Major League Dodgers at the beginning of the 1948 season, but Branch Rickey wanted him to break the color line of the American Association, one of the top Minor Leagues. Rickey sent him to play for a Dodgers team in that league, the one in St. Paul, Minnesota.

"Just be Roy Campanella," Rickey said, "and everything will be all right."

Rickey was right. Campanella was the same happy, friendly man he had always been, the same terrific ballplayer, and the fans in St. Paul loved him.

"I've got news for you, Roy," the team's manager told him on June 30, 1948, "bad for me, but good for you."

Campanella was leaving the St. Paul team. He was moving back to the Brooklyn Dodgers.

In early July, when Campy rejoined the team, it was near the bottom of the league. He got three hits in each of the next three games, nine hits in all, two of them home runs. The team started winning and ended the season in third place. The next year, Campy's first full year on the Dodgers, the team finished first in the National League.

Campy was a great player on one of baseball's very best teams.

He was chosen the league's all-star catcher eight years in a row. In 1951, 1953, and 1955, he was chosen as the league's Most Valuable Player. In five of the ten years Campy played for the Dodgers, the team finished first in the National League. Each time they faced the New York Yankees in the World Series.

Among Campy's real thrills was playing in the 1955 World Series. He hit a home run in his first at bat in the series. In the final game, he doubled and scored the first run. The team won that game and the series, the Dodgers' first World Series win.

The fans loved Roy Campanella, and he loved the game. "To play in the big leagues, you got to be a man," he said, "but you got to have a lot of little boy in you, too."

He was proud to be baseball's first African American catcher, but, "When I'm hitting or catching," he once said, "I don't think of the color of my skin." He hoped fans would feel that way, too, and most of them did.

He knew his baseball career would one day end, and he had a family to support. So in 1951 he opened a wine and liquor store in New York City. Early in the morning, on January 28, 1958, he was leaving it.

"I was tired and it was cold and late, but I drove carefully," he later wrote. "There were big patches of ice in the road. . . . I suddenly lost control. The car wouldn't behave. . . . I fought the wheel. The brakes were useless. . . . I saw this telephone pole right where I was headed. . . . I just did hit it. . . . The car bounced off and turned completely over, landing on its right side."

The first days after the accident "were the worst of my life," he later wrote. "I thought I was a goner." He couldn't walk or hold a ball, and at first, he didn't want to see anyone, not even his children. Soon, though, his attitude changed. He compared the fight ahead to baseball. "When you're in a slump, you don't feel sorry for yourself. . . . You don't quit."

He practiced sitting in a wheelchair and then moving around in it. He learned to feed himself. He started working at getting better, and he was happy again.

After a hospital visit, a friend of teammate Carl Erskine said, "I thought we went there to cheer him up. He made me feel terrific."

Campanella never played or walked again, but he never lost his love for baseball.

Just a few months after his accident, he was in bed, flat on his back, looking up at a mirror pointed to a television so he could watch a Dodgers game. Campy still had a good eye for detail, and after the game, with some help, he called his friend and former teammate Charlie Neal. "Charlie," he said, "you're never going to start hitting again unless you pull that right foot back about six inches."

Neal followed Campanella's advice, and his hitting improved.

Soon Roy Campanella was a Dodgers spring training coach. He worked with the team's new catcher, Johnny Roseboro.

He had a radio program, *Campy's Corner*, and his own television show, and he held baseball clinics for teenagers.

"He was still Campy," Yankees catcher Yogi Berra later said, "still a special person. He'd always have that big smile despite what happened to him."

In 1969, Roy Campanella, one of baseball's most beloved players, was given the sport's greatest honor. He was elected to its Hall of Fame.

Roy Campanella, once a hero on the baseball fields, became a hero off the field. People everywhere read newspaper and magazine articles about how he faced his disabilities with courage and good humor.

In his autobiography, *It's Good to Be Alive*, he called his life exciting and wonderful—"a life such as few people have been fortunate enough to live."

The first Thanksgiving after his accident, he counted his blessings. "I just can't begin to tell you how lucky I am," he said. "I'm thankful just to be home with my family."

Roy Campanella's determination and good cheer lifted the spirit of people with disabilities.

Just over a year after his accident, he met an old woman with braces on both of her legs. "I came a long way," she told him, "to see you and thank you, for you gave me the courage and the will to go on."

"We're a rugged breed," Campy once said of the disabled. "Sure I'd love to walk. Sure I would. But I'm not going to worry myself to death because I can't."

Together with his third wife, Roxie, he set up the Roy and Roxie Campanella Physical Therapy Scholarship Foundation. It provides equipment, support, and encouragement for people with disabilities like Campy's and help for people studying to work with the disabled.

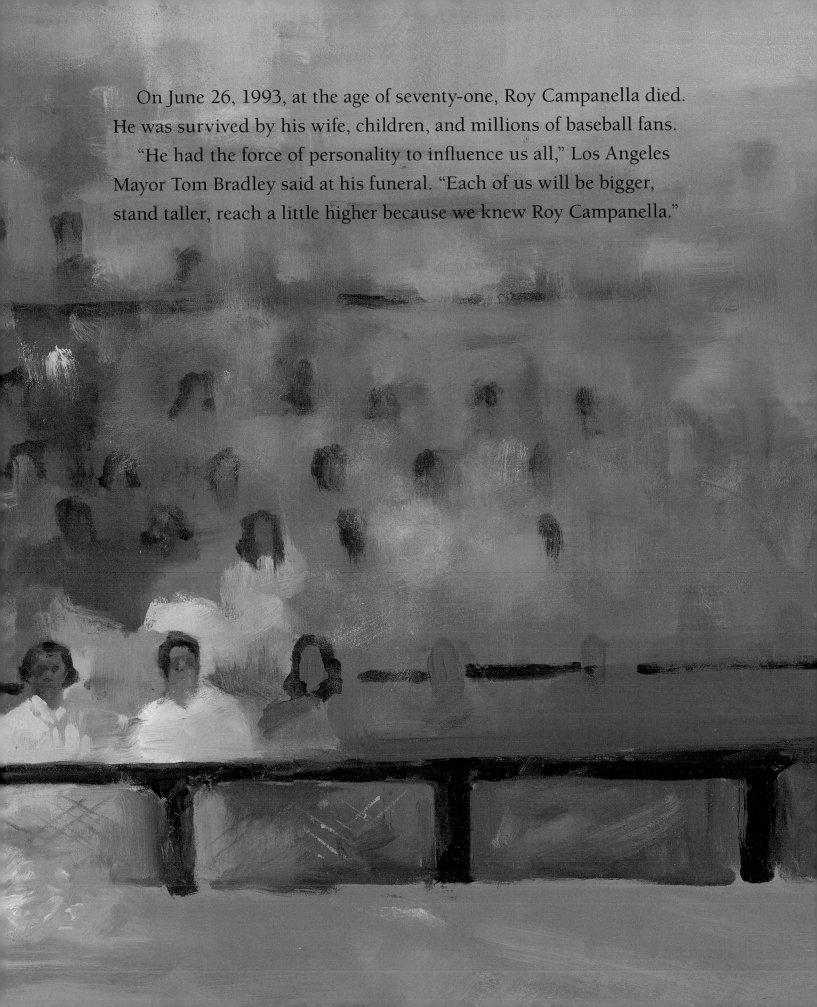

On June 26, 1993, at the age of seventy-one, Roy Campanella died.
He was survived by his wife, children, and millions of baseball fans.
"He had the force of personality to influence us all," Los Angeles
Mayor Tom Bradley said at his funeral. "Each of us will be bigger,
stand taller, reach a little higher because we knew Roy Campanella."

Important Dates:

1921 Born in Homestead, Pennsylvania, November 19.

1937 Joins the Baltimore Elite Giants, a professional team.

Quits school to play baseball, November 20.

1948 Joins the Brooklyn Dodgers.

1951 Wins the first of three Most Valuable Player Awards as a Brooklyn Dodger.

1955 Brooklyn Dodgers win their only World Series, October 4.

1957 Brooklyn Dodgers play their last game at Ebbets Field.

1958 Left paralyzed by an automobile accident, January 28.

Dodgers move to California and become the Los Angeles Dodgers.

1959 Roy Campanella night at the Los Angeles Coliseum, May 7.

1969 Elected to baseball's Hall of Fame.

1993 Dies in Los Angeles, California, June 26.

2006 The U.S. Postal Service issues a 39-cent postage stamp of Campanella as one of the "Baseball Sluggers" along with Mickey Mantle, Hank Greenberg, and Mel Ott.

Quotes:

"The sight . . . anything like it." Campanella, *It's Good to Be Alive*, p. 298.

"To do that . . . earn his way," ibid, p. 72.

"Your record . . . with people," ibid, p. 109.

"Play for me," *New York Post*, June 28, 1993.

"I'll beat you to a pulp." Campanella, *It's Good to Be Alive*, p. 124.

"Just be . . . all right," ibid, p. 141.

"I've got . . . for you," ibid, p. 143.

"To play . . . in you, too," *New York Times*, June 28, 1993.

"When I'm . . . my skin," *New York Post*, June 28, 1993.

"I was tired . . . right side," Campanella, *It's Good to Be Alive*, pp. 18–19.

"were the worst . . . life," ibid, p. 202.

"I thought . . . goner," ibid.

"When you're in . . . don't quit," ibid, p. 206.

"I thought . . . feel terrific," Erskine, *Tales from the Dodger Dugout*, p. 98.

"Charlie . . . six inches," *New York Times*, March 1, 1959.

"He was still . . . him," correspondence, Yogi Berra, October 25, 2004.

"a life . . . live," Campanella, *It's Good to Be Alive*, p. 3.

"I just can't . . . with my family," *New York Times*, November 27, 1958.

"I came . . . to go on," Campanella, *It's Good to Be Alive*, p. 4.

"We're a rugged breed . . . I can't," Tackach, *Roy Campanella*, p. 56

"He had . . . we knew Roy Campanella," *New York Post*, July 1, 1993.

Suggested Reading:

Campanella, Roy. *It's Good to Be Alive*. Boston: Little, Brown and Company, 1959.

Drysdale, Don, with Bob Verdi. *Once a Bum, Always a Dodger*. New York: St. Martin's Press, 1990.

Erskine, Carl. *Tales from the Dodger Dugout*. Champaign, Ill.: Sports Publications, 2000.

McKissack, Patricia C., and Fredrick McKissack, Jr. *Black Diamond: The Story of the Negro Baseball Leagues*. New York: Scholastic, 1994.

Tackach, James. *Roy Campanella*. New York: Chelsea House Publishers, 1991.

Author correspondence with Yogi Berra, October 25, 2004.

Amsterdam News, *LIFE* magazine, *Los Angeles Times*, *New York Post*, *New York Times*, *Newsday*, and *U.S.A. Today Baseball Weekly*.

www.RoyCampanella.com

www.baseballhalloffame.org

www.thebaseballpage.com